TRUTH or POOP?

BOOK ONE
AMAZING ANIMALS

James Warwood

Truth or Poop?

BOOK ONE
AMAZING ANIMALS

Paperback ISBN: 9798466598995
Ebook ASIN: B09CL5QLHP
Audiobook: B09ML25JPT

Cover art by James Warwood
Edited by Anne Chilcott
Interior design by James Warwood

www.cjwarwood.com

Give feedback on the book at:
me@cjwarwood.com

First Edition

For my two boys,

(who are little poop machines, but will one day hopefully enjoy this book).

Contents

Introduction

WELCOME TO TRUTH OR POOP!

This is a true or false quiz book series and book one is all about amazing animals. Inside these pages you'll be treated to fifty wild and wacky facts. From frogs to dogs, dolphins to pigeons, bats to cats (and even rats). It's your job to sort the fact from the fib, the real from the fake . . .

The TRUTH from the POOP.

RULES OF THE GAME

Each chapter will start with a fact.

Be warned . . . it might sound incredibly silly or perfectly logically but take a breath and engage your brain cells. Think it through. Then you'll be asked the golden question:

That's when you need to make a decision and stick with it. Then, turn the page and find out if you're a genius in the making or the book has managed to trick you. If the fact is as real as the sun in the sky, you'll see a big thumbs up:

If the fact is as made-up as a leprechaun riding a unicorn through the Forbidden Forest, you'll see a cheeky poop:

Count how many you get right as you go. Then, once you've got to the end, post how many you got correct as a review (and, while you're there, why not suggest what the theme of the next book should be).

RIGHT THEN, ARE YOU READY?

Good.

Let's start with chickens.

FACT #1
Chickens

The closest living relative to the T-Rex is a chicken.

Turns out dinosaurs are more bird than reptile.

For decades, dinosaurs were thought to be reptiles: big ones, but also cold-blooded, slow-moving, and dim-witted. Then a big discovery was made . . . by mistake. Scientists discovered a complete T-Rex bone. Faced with flying a giant femur out of a remote Montana field site, they broke the bone in half so it would fit inside their helicopter. In doing so they discovered molecules of collagen, a structural protein that appears in slightly different forms in many animals.

They compared the dinosaur version with 21 living animals, including humans, chimps, mice, chickens, ostriches, alligators, and salmon. The chicken was almost identical. They've even taken this further by strapping a replica T-Rex tail to chickens to study how the dinosaur may have moved around.

Poor chickens. It's entirely possible that dinosaur meat tastes like chicken too. Everything else does, right? Just imagine the size of a finger-licking T-Rex drumstick. It could feed an entire village.

FACT #2
Cows

Cows can sleep standing up, but they can only dream lying down.

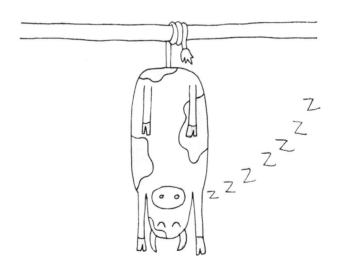

is it TRUTH or POOP?

Cows do sleep standing up, but they don't experience full REM sleep (the deep slumber of Rapid Eye Movement is what allows us to dream).

Most four-legged land herbivores — cows, moose, rhinos, bison, and horses — can doze lightly on their feet, but they have to lie down to get a proper good night's sleep. Their limbs contain tendons and ligaments that allow them to remain standing with minimal muscular effort. This allows them to stand and even doze for long periods.

So, the next time you spot cows in a field on a car journey, see if you can tell which ones have drifted off for a quick nap.

FACT #3
Armadillos

An armadillo's armour is bulletproof.

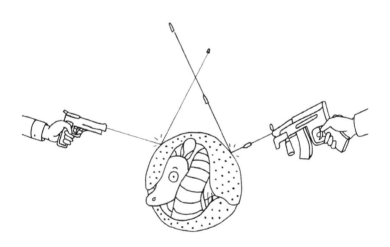

is it TRUTH or POOP?

it's POOP

They might look it, but the armour of an armadillo is not bulletproof.

The armadillo has a protective bony armour, called the osteoderm, which moulds to its shell-like skin. The top layer of the shell is made of a layer of *keratin*: an extremely useful protein that makes up hair, nails, and horns. Beneath the keratin there is another layer of hexagonal tiles that are almost identical to bones. Fibres connect the tiles, allowing for flexibility in the armour. It might not be bulletproof, but the armadillo's armour has inspired researchers to create a protective material out of glass plates segmented into hexagons and set atop a soft vest.

The material turned out to be 70% more puncture-resistant than a solid plate of the same thickness. Don't underestimate this little critter, as there have been reports that bullets have ricocheted off the hardy creatures. In fact, a man from Texas once fired a revolver at one and it bounced back and hit him in the face.

Serves him right! Unless the armadillo stole the TV Remote, then the guy had it coming.

FACT #4

Bats

A bat can eat up to 1,000 insects per hour.

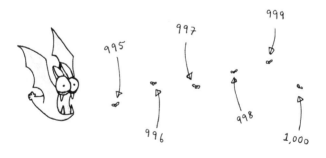

is it TRUTH or POOP?

it's TRUTH

Each night bats can eat their body weight or more in insects.

That's somewhere in the region of 600 to 1,000 insects. They eat moths, crickets, locusts, fruit flies, gnats, beetles, mosquitoes, and other little bugs. And because bats eat so many insects, which have exoskeletons made of a shiny material called chitin, some bat poop sparkles.

So, the next time you see a shiny cave – it's probably a toilet for bats.

FACT #5
Dolphins

Wild dolphins call each other by name.

it's TRUTH 👍

Dolphins use a unique whistle to identify each other. Scientists have noticed that a dolphin will respond when it hears the sound of its own signature whistle, repeating that whistle back in a way that seems to say, "Yup, I'm here—did you call my name?" So, just like us humans, if they hear their name, they answer.

Who knows what they talk about after that? The weather? The latest marine gossip? Whether the water is feeling warmer or did someone just have a wee?

FACT #6
Ducks

Ducks can surf.

it's TRUTH

On California's beaches, mallard ducks have learned to surf for food.

As the swash (the part of a broken wave that washes up a beach) approaches the mallards from behind, the duck is lifted up, transported by the wave, and then dropped off further down the beach. The bird then plunges its bill in the loose sand, waggles it around, and catches a Pacific sand crab. Once they've eaten the tasty reward, they do it all over again. But aren't mallards freshwater birds? What are they doing surfing? Scientists can only guess that they saw shorebirds wading in the swash and thought they could give that a go.

What next?

Will a duck see someone rollerblading and swap the surfboard for wheels?

FACT #7

Pigeons

Pigeons can do math.

it's TRUTH

No, really. Pigeons are brilliant at simple maths.

Many animals, from honeybees to elephants, can tell the difference between quantities of items, sounds, or smells. But only primates (all species, from lemurs to chimpanzees) were known to be able to reason numerically, until the pigeon rocked up to the lab. Scientists gave the pigeons three images containing one, two, or three objects. All three images appeared at once on a touch screen and the pigeons pecked the screen to make a response. If they correctly accomplished the task, pecking the images in ascending order, they received a wheat snack.

They then went even further and presented the pigeons with pairs of images containing 1, 2, 3, 4, 5, 6, 7, 8, or 9 objects. The pigeons again had to pair the items in ascending order. For example, if a pigeon saw 8 and 5, it had to peck the objects representing 5 first. Amazingly, the pigeons matched the mathematical skills of the monkeys.

So, if you spot a monkey in a huff on the next nature show you watch, you'll know why.

FACT #8
The Fastest

Ostriches can run faster than greyhounds dogs, hares can run faster than ostriches, horses can run faster than hares, but the horsefly will beat them all!

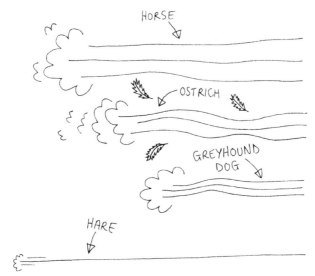

It might surprise you to learn that, although the horsefly is the fastest on this list, the next fastest only has two legs.

Traditionally, it's thought that having four legs makes you a much faster runner, but no one told the Ostriches. You want proof? Then here are the top speeds for the fastest land animals:

- Cheetah = 105kph (65mph)
- Pronghorn Antelope = 100kph (62mph)
- Springbok Antelope = 97kph (60mph)
- Ostrich = 97kph (60mph)
- Horse = 88kph (55mph)
- Brown Hare = 77kph (48mph)
- Greyhound Dog = 74kph (46mph)

Way down the list comes another two-legged animal that can reach speeds of 38kph (23mph). That was the fastest man to run the 100m sprint – Usain Bolt.

And a very humbling thing it is, to think that a horsefly can do the 100m sprint four times over in the time it took the fastest man on earth.

FACT #9
Zebras

Zebra stripes act as a natural bug repellent (even painting cows works too).

it's TRUTH

Zebra stripes confuse bugs, causing them to abort a landing.

We used to think that the bold patterns confuse predators, or that they keep the animals cool. But the stripy mystery has now been solved. Scientists covered nine horses with three different coats, one black, one white, and one striped much like a zebra. The zebra stripes did not deter flies from afar; both zebras and uncovered domestic horses experienced the same rate of circling flies. But a close analysis of the flies' final approach to the striped animals revealed the insects failed to decelerate, and instead flew over the stripes or bumped into them.

The scientists did not see a single insect bite on the zebra's skin, whereas the flies successfully did so 239 times on the uncovered horses. Only five flies landed on the horses dressed in zebra coats, whereas over 60 touched down on those in the solid black and solid white coats in the same time period.

Business idea: full-body zebra suits with zebra face paint. Suck on that annoying little fly.

FACT #10
Worms

Some worms can jump.

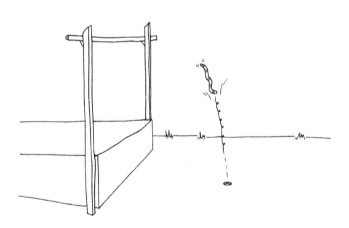

is it TRUTH or POOP?

Specifically, it's the Asian jumping worm that can spring into the air.

Also known as crazy worms, Alabama jumpers and snake worms, they get their name from their behaviour when picked up. They will violently thrash and spring into the air, leaping back onto the ground. Despite this amazing skill, they are seen as a pest because they ravenously feed on the nutrients plants and fungi need to survive. They also have a curious defence mechanism where they can shed their tails to escape. The purpose being to leave a light snack for their predator to munch on while they make their escape. Be thankful us humans never developed a similar tactic.

Just imagine that, seeing a lion licking his lips and then having to hop away because one of your legs has fallen off.

FACT #11
Birds

Birds are immune to the heat of chili peppers.

VINDALOO

is it **TRUTH** or **POOP?**

it's **TRUTH** 👍

Birds biologically cannot taste *capsaicin* – the chemical that makes peppers feel 'hot' in your mouth.

The Carolina Reaper is the hottest pepper in the world. It's 200 times hotter than a Jalapeño. The little red firecracker should be sold with several ice lollies and a doctor's note. But for birds, it's just another snack. Why? Because they have considerably fewer tastebuds. A chicken has just 24 taste buds, and pigeons have 37, compared to 10,000 currently in your mouth.

It's thought that hot pepper plants become selective about the animals that eat their fruit (oh, yes, and peppers are a fruit, weird, I know). These plants want their fruit to be eaten by birds as the seeds can survive through their digestive system as they fly for miles, then do their morning business on your neighbour's car. Let that be a lesson to us all, bird poo is probably the hottest hot sauce nature has created.

So, don't go smearing it in a sandwich (unless it's your older brother's).

FACT #12
Cats

While trying to find a cure for AIDS, scientists made glow-in-the-dark cats.

is it **TRUTH** or **POOP?**

it's

Yep, it sounds crazy but glow-in-the-dark cats really have been genetically engineered.

Let me try to explain this one. By attaching an easily identifiable marker to a gene, scientists can determine whether it has been successfully introduced into an animal's DNA. In 2011 scientists at the Mayo clinic used a fluorescent protein from a specific jellyfish when testing an anti-FIV (the cat equivalent of AIDS) gene. The tests were a success, but the cats ended up glowing in the dark thanks to the extra bit of jellyfish now inside their DNA make-up. In fact, even the offspring of these cats glow-in-the-dark! Their success is just one step along the way to an ultimate cure for AIDS.

I'm pretty sure you can't request this extra feature from your local pet shop, but I think you'll agree it's worth a try if your parents are thinking of getting a cat.

FACT #13

Owls

10% of mated barn owls ended in divorce, compared to 37% in humans in 2020 in the USA.

In fact, it's much higher.

Many birds are monogamous (which means they find a mate and stick with them for life), including owls, ducks, swans, and geese. But it's not all cooing and cuddling in the nest. Even in the wild, marriage doesn't always work out. 23.5% of Barn Owls decide to split up and find a different partner. Successful barn owls will have two broods a year with about six eggs in a single brood. While many barn owl pairs will stick it out for the long haul, the ones to call it quits do so if they find that they're not having enough chicks together.

Still, they have a better chance of staying together than humans, with a 37% divorce rate recorded in the USA in 2020.

FACT #14
Dogs

During World War II, they awarded a Great Dane named Juliana the Blue Cross Medal.

it's  TRUTH 👍

Juliana was a war hero, and not just once.

In 1941, two years into World War II, the Germans were dropping incendiary bombs across Britain. They were designed to start devastating fires in key locations of the war effort. One such bomb fell through the roof of the house in which Juliana and her owner lived. The Great Dane stood over the live explosive and unleashed a golden shower that extinguished the incendiary bomb. That's right, the dog saved the day by peeing on it! That's how she got her first Blue Cross Medal for bravery, but she went on to earn another three years later. When a fire broke out in her owner's shoe shop, Juliana alerted the entire family of the danger so that everyone escaped with their lives.

What an amazing dog. She was truly a Great Dane with a great bladder!

FACT #15

Orangutans

Orangutans build nests.

is it TRUTH or POOP?

it's TRUTH 👍

Orangutans like to be comfortable, and so will make a lovely nest rather than roughing it on the forest floor.

The orange primates make a sleeping platform, or nest, every single night. They do this by pulling several large branches together, using smaller branches for a mattress, and binding the structure together by weaving in more supple branches. In wet weather, they sometimes even add a roof. As orangutans make a new nest to sleep in every night, biologists actually use their nests to estimate their population size. They count nests both from the ground and the air as they're much easier to spot than the elusive hairy creatures.

At least you know who to ask to make you a bed if you're ever stranded in the Amazon Rainforest (don't bother asking an anaconda, they'll squeeze you dry).

FACT #16
Rhino's

A rhino's horn is made from the same stuff as our fingernails.

it's  👍

The horn of a rhino is very similar to your fingernails. Weird, I know, but it's true.

A rhino's horn is made of tightly wrapped strands of *keratin* — the same protein which forms the basis of our hair and nails. Animal claws and hooves, bird feathers, porcupine quills, and the shells of tortoises are also made of keratin. Rhinos are the only animal to have a horn that is entirely made from keratin; unlike those of cattle, sheep, antelopes, and giraffes, they don't have any bone core. Their horns grow continuously during their lifetime, much like our fingers and toenails.

The white rhino's horn can grow 7 cm every year, and the record length is 150 cm long (which is the size of a quarter of a giraffe, half as tall as a London bus, and one whole Danny DeVito).

FACT #17
Buffalos

African buffalo herds display voting behaviour.

it's TRUTH 👍

Buffalos are among the animals who run their own little democracies.

African buffalo are herd herbivores that often make group decisions about when and where to move. In the 1990s, researchers realised that what initially looked like a really good stretch was actually a type of voting-related behaviour, in which females show their travel preferences by standing up, staring in one direction, and then lying back down. What makes this even more interesting is that only the adult females have a say. That's right, the opposite way round to how it used to be in western human society, where women were not allowed to vote. Other animals that make big decisions democratically include meerkats, pigeons, and honeybees.

So then, democracy is not unique to Homo sapiens americanus (that's Latin for us humans), who arguably do democracy much worse than our neighbours in the animal kingdom.

FACT #18
Hummingbirds

Hummingbirds are the only known birds that can fly backwards.

is it TRUTH or POOP?

it's TRUTH 👍

The only birds that can fly backwards for any length of time are hummingbirds.

Unlike other birds, hummingbirds have a rotator cuff, like humans, that supports and strengthens the shoulder joint and allows the hummingbird's wings to move in a figure of eight motion. This adaptation to manoeuvre their wings in such a way is what gives these remarkable, small birds the ability to fly in any direction they want (up, down, forwards, backwards, side to side, hover, and even upside down.) Hummingbirds beat their wings about 8 to 200 times per second. The typical hummingbird flight is at a speed of 30 miles per hour. However, during the courtship ritual, the male bird can dive at a stunning speed of 60 miles per hour. An average bird has about 1000 to 1500 feathers, which is much less than the feathers of other birds. This reduces the weight of the average hummingbird and makes it easier for it to fly.

A typical hummingbird weighs close to a mere three grams. That's roughly the same as a single penny. Do you know how many pennies the average human weighs? 26,666 pennies!

FACT #19

Ostriches

Ostriches legs are so powerful that their kicks can kill a lion.

is it TRUTH or POOP?

it's TRUTH 👍

A nd not just a lion, an ostrich could even take out a human in one kick!

Ostriches are the largest and heaviest birds in the world. Although they cannot fly, ostriches make it up for it with their powerful legs. The ostrich relies on its muscular legs—uniquely two-toed, with the main toe developed almost as a hoof and a 4-inch claw—to escape its enemies. They are also the fastest running birds, reaching speeds of up to 60 mph. At this speed, they are the only animals that can outrun leopards. Ostrich brains are around the same size as a walnut and smaller than their eyes. Their tiny brains mean they are not particularly intelligent, but with the largest eyeball of any bird, they can see as far as 2.2 miles.

Congrats to the ostrich. They're both the deadliest and dumbest birds in the world.

FACT #20
Wombats

During bushfires, wombat burrows become places of shelter for many other animals.

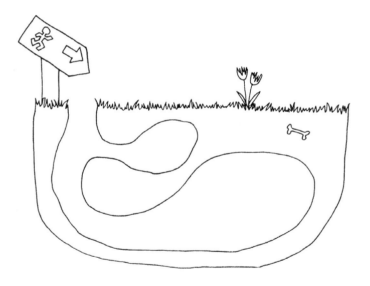

it's TRUTH 👍

These friendly creatures are the refugee welcomers of the animal kingdom.

Wombat burrows, known as warrens, can be huge! These underground homes can contain tunnels over 200 metres long. And these warrens don't just serve as homes for wombats – they can become vital shelters for other small mammals, too. Wombats are only found in Australia, which can experience extreme heat that can cause fires to break out. During bushfires, the tunnels stay cool, offering protection from the flames. Rock wallabies, bettongs, skinks, and even little penguins have been seen using wombat warrens to escape fires or hide from predators. And the warrens are deep enough to be completely fireproof so that after a bushfire, a wombat can munch on roots and bark in the earth until the grass regrows on the surface.

Good to know that, if you're ever caught in a bushfire in the outback of Australia, you know which creature to ask for shelter.

FACT #21
Elephants

There are three species of elephant, not two.

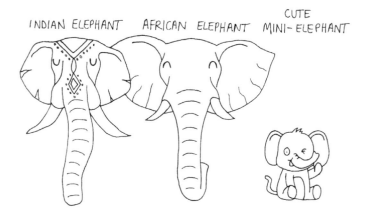

INDIAN ELEPHANT · AFRICAN ELEPHANT · CUTE MINI-ELEPHANT

is it TRUTH or POOP?

it's **TRUTH** 👍

For a long time, there were only two – African elephants and Asian elephants – but now there's a new kid on the block.

Until recently, African forest elephants were thought to be a subspecies of the African elephant, but new research discovered that they are actually a separate species entirely. These elephants live in the tropical forests of Africa's Congo Basin. They have straighter tusks and more rounded ears than savannah elephants. Who knows how many more undiscovered species there might be out there in plain sight? It is thought that an average of 50 new plant and animal species are discovered every day!

If you work hard in school and fancy going on a crazy expedition to the Amazon Rain Forrest or the Sahara Desert, you could make an amazing discovery yourself.

FACT #22
Squirrels

Hundreds of trees get planted every year because of squirrels forgetting where they buried their nuts.

it's

You may have heard this fact before, that squirrels forget where they hide half of their nuts, but it turns out this is simply just not the case.

The reality is that squirrels are very good at remembering where they stash their nuts. The reason that this theory is widely believed is that they rarely collect all their nuts. Not because they can't remember where they put them, but because they prepare for the worst-case scenario. Squirrels will over-stock their hidden stash of nuts for two reasons. First, they never know if it will be a long winter, so having the extra food source is a matter of life and death. And second, other crafty animals will often take advantage of the organised little critters and dig up a few of their nuts.

Squirrels aren't forgetful after all. Planting new trees is just a happy side-effect. Thanks, squirrels!

FACT #23

Flamingos

Flamingos eat with their heads upside down.

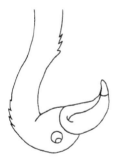

is it TRUTH or POOP?

it's **TRUTH** 👍

That's right, the pink birds prefer to dip their heads into the water upside down to have a snack.

Flamingos are filter feeders. That means that when they walk around in the shallow waters, they're actually mixing up the little animals and nutrients that are in the mud. The birds will plunge their neck down under the water with their head upside down, then close their mouth and force the water through comb-like extensions on their beak, using their tongue to push the water out while keeping all the food in. Flamingos don't even care what they find, whatever goes in they'll eat: crustaceans, worms, algae, insects, shrimps, plant material, and even fish.

I wouldn't recommend giving it a go, though. Your parents might give you a funny look if you ask for permission to eat your dinner in the bath.

FACT #24

Hippos

Hippos can run faster than humans.

it's TRUTH

Yep, they might be fat, but they're also fast!

Hippos are the second-largest land animal, second only to elephants. Male hippos can weigh over 6,000 pounds, but despite their massive bulk, hippos can run faster than humans — up to 30 miles per hour compared to the average human at 15 miles per hour! As hippos are extremely territorial, they charge at anyone who comes between them and water. Every year it's estimated that they kill the most humans in Africa at somewhere between 500-1000. If you are an elite athlete, then you might stand a chance of surviving seeing as hippos have poor stamina and can only run at full speed for 30 seconds.

The best thing to do is to run away from the water. And if you've got a jet pack, that would be even better.

FACT #25

Dogs

It has been documented that some dogs have hypnotised their owners.

is it **TRUTH** or **POOP?**

it's POOP

Don't be silly! Dogs can't hypnotise humans but turn that sentence around and it becomes a truth.

Apparently, chickens are the easiest animal to hypnotise, but it is also possible to do it to dogs, cats, horses, cows, and even frogs. So, now I'm guessing you want to know how it's done. First, make sure your dog is in a calm and safe environment, their dog bed would do nicely. Gently stroke your dog on their head, back, and belly. Then repeat a soothing phrase to keep them relaxed, try 'good dog' or just the word 'relax'. It could take 10 minutes or 10 seconds, but your dog could already be hypnotised (or just super chilled out). For a deeper state of hypnosis, try shifting your dog into a submissive state. If you have a small dog, try putting them on your lap with their bottom closest to you and their head between your knees. If you have a large dog, move your dog on their back and continue to stroke their belly until their legs go limp.

The aim is to get them into a state known as tonic immobility. Their limbs will be perfectly still and limp. You can test it by gently moving their legs and, if they are hypnotised, they won't react. To wake them from the state of hypnosis, a loud clap or a decisive call will get them up and moving again.

FACT #26
Cats

A cat has 32 muscles in each ear.

is it TRUTH or POOP?

it's **TRUTH** 👍

That's a lot of muscles for one ear. But they come in pretty handy.

Cats have 32 ear muscles, which allow them to swivel and rotate to pinpoint the source of a noise. And that's not all, they can also move each ear independently and rotate them 180 degrees. Your feline friend can also hear higher and lower frequencies than humans (and dogs), which helps them find their prey. What you probably don't realise is that your cat also uses its ears to communicate with other cats and with you.

If you have a pet cat, go take a look at their ears. If they are pointing up and facing forwards, then your cat is happy and wants to be stroked. If they are laying down, then keep your hands to yourself, unless you want to be bitten.

FACT #27

Snakes

Even when a snake has its eyes closed, it can still see through its eyelids.

is it TRUTH or POOP?

it's **TRUTH** 👍

That's right, the legless reptiles are even freakier than you might think.

Technically, snakes have no eyelids. Instead, they have a thin clear membrane that covers their eyes. And get this, they're called spectacles. The membrane is attached to their skin, which means they can't blink. It comes in handy seeing as they live close to the ground. They get dust, grit, and bits of vegetation in their faces as they slither around. The spectacles protect their eyes from getting scratched. A thin layer of tear-like fluid separates the membrane from the eye. Scientists are studying snake eyes to improve contact lenses.

The next time you go to the zoo, and it looks like a snake is staring at you, it could be having a nap inside.

FACT #28

Reindeer

Reindeer have beards.

is it **TRUTH** or **POOP?**

it's TRUTH

You know Dasher and Dancer and Comet and Vixen, but do you know reindeer grow beards in the winter?

Reindeer must cope with some serious climate changes. They have to adapt to changes in temperature, from -70 degrees in the winter to +40 degrees in the summer. When temperatures become extremely cold, they lower the temperature in their legs to near freezing levels in order to keep their core body heat up. For winter grazing they grow facial hair long enough to cover their mouths so that it protects their muzzles from the snow. When the temperatures swing the other way, they shed their winter coat to reveal a fine summer coat. Reindeer also have ultraviolet vision which allows them to find food even under 60 cm of snow.

So, reindeer are very similar to dads: they can both grow beards, find snacks where no one else can, and often look completely ridiculous.

FACT #29

Sloths, Moths and Algae

Sloths, moths, and algae all live together in harmony.

it's

So, they haven't moved into a downtown apartment together, but they are still inseparable.

The pyralid moth is a species of moth that lives in the sloth's fleece. Right next to them is a species of algae that grows in the grooved hair of the sloth. It's a curious relationship that has made many scientists scratch their heads. The most likely explanation is that the moth transports nutrient-rich poop from the sloth's waste to fertilise the algae. In other words, the moths are algae farmers that live on the sloth's back. And that's not the end of the strange story. The algae make for a tasty snack for the sloth rich in important nutrients!

We can learn something from the animal kingdom. There's nothing better than a friend unless it's a friend with algae.

FACT #30
Camels

The only known animals in the world that will eat a cactus are camels.

it's  POOP

The prickly things might look inedible, but there are quite a few animals that will munch on them (including us humans).

It's a bit of a trick question, because like some other flowering plants, cacti can grow fruit. It's the fruit that many animals will happily eat all day long. But camels are the only animals that eat the entire cactus, needles and all. How do they do it? They have something called papillae inside their mouths, which look like wiggly little fingers. The papillae direct the sharp needles so that they slide down to the stomach vertically, therefore stopping them from being poked by the nasty thorns. And guess what the papillae are made from. Yep, it's that wonderful protein that keeps on turning up to this wild party – *keratin*. Then, when their stomachs are full of needles, billions of bacteria break them down.

The funniest thing about this fact is that the thorny cactus causes some pain to the camels. However, they choose to push through the pain just to get to the juicy, tasty part.

FACT #31
Kangaroos

Kangaroos can't walk backwards.

it's  TRUTH

Skippy can hop forwards, left and right, but he can't hop backwards if he drops his keys. But why can't they do something that seems so simple?

Well, there are two reasons: the structure of their powerful back feet and their large tails. The kangaroo has perfected jumping, and we call the movement *saltatory locomotion*. With huge back feet and a long tail as a counterbalance, they can jump up to thirty feet in a single leap. They can also move from side to side with amazing agility, but they cannot jump backwards because their thick, muscular tail acts as a handbrake. Their long feet and heavy tail also make walking impossible, forward or backward. But don't feel too sorry for them.

It's also the reason you'll find a kangaroo on the Australian Coat of Arms — the designers wanted to symbolise the way the nation was only moving forward, so they picked an animal that physically can't move backwards.

FACT #32

Crows

Crows use cars to open nuts.

These clever birds are cracking nuts in very unnatural ways.

Ever been to Japan? Site of the Olympic Games in 2020, the birthplace of karate, sushi, and the only place in the world that has a tourist attraction island populated with cuddly rabbits (but I'll leave that 'Truth or Poop' for another book). Japanese crows have learned to drop nuts in the middle of a busy road so that cars will run them over and crack them open. But perhaps most amazing of all, the crows have learned the traffic lights system in Japan so that they know when it's safe to lay out the nuts, and when it's safe to hop down and gobble them up.

What next? Will the crows start leaving packets of crisps on the road too, and fizzy drinks bottles when they're thirsty for pop?

FACT #33

Elephants

Elephants can't jump.

it's TRUTH 👍

Yep, that's one thing worms can do better than elephants.

If you think about it, this one makes sense. Elephants can grow over 3 metres tall and can weigh up to 6 tonnes. That's around the same weight as the average delivery truck and you don't see them hopping around to deliver parcels, do ya? In fact, it's even estimated that the T-Rex weighed about the same as the heaviest living elephant. Researchers at the Royal Veterinary College in London have studied the elephant's inability to jump and put the blame on their, and I quote, "wimpy lower-leg muscles" and "inflexible ankles". Having wimpy legs also makes it difficult for them to run for more than a short distance.

Poor animals. They'll never get to experience the joy of jumping in puddles, especially as they'd be able to make the most epic splashes. Shall we all chip in together and buy them a giant trampoline?

FACT #34
Penguins

There's an abandoned minefield that has accidentally created a penguin sanctuary.

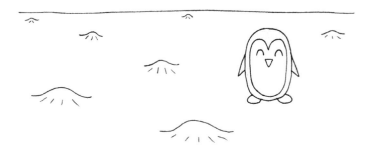

it's TRUTH 👍

The world's largest penguin sanctuary isn't a protected national park or reserve, but a minefield.

When Argentina invaded the Falklands in 1982, they laid tens of thousands of landmines to defend strategic locations against the coming British attempt to retake the islands. One such location, Yorke Bay, was peppered with some 20,000 landmines and many of the landmines across the island are fenced off and well-marked to stop humans wandering in. But it didn't stop the penguins. Too light to set off the landmines, they could walk around, breed, and frolic behind the barbed wire fences and danger signs.

The beach is home to 5 penguin species — gentoo, southern rockhopper, magellanic, king, and macaroni — all waddling about without a care in the world. Strangely, the locals aren't that bothered that they share their island with thousands of landmines. One islander is quoted to have said "since the mines have been here, I have only ever known 2 of my 8,000 sheep to get blown up."

So, if you were wondering which is heavier – a sheep or a penguin – now you know that too.

FACT #35

Dogs

Your dog probably dreams about you.

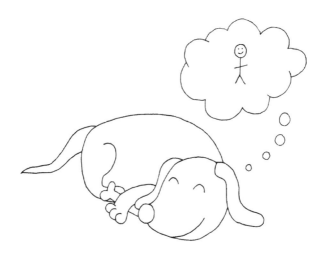

it's

Oh yes. There are scientists out there, somewhere, who have the time and gained the funding to work out what dogs dream about . . . and it turns out it's probably you.

Like all mammals (including us) dogs have a sleep cycle where they have periods of deep sleep when the brain is less active and then into periods of Rapid Eye Movement (REM) sleep when dreams occur for humans. Scientists think there is every reason to think that dogs dream too and because our everyday experiences often end up in our dreams, it's safe to say that dogs dream about their owner's face, of their smell, and of pleasing or annoying them. So, what about cats? Do they dream about their owners too? One scientist was able to switch off a part of a cat's brain that stops movement during sleep. The cat lay quietly through the other stages of sleep, and when REM began, it leaped up, stalked, pounced, arched its back, and hissed. What was it doing in its sleep? Probably hunting a mouse, or possibly their owner?

There you go. Dogs and cats both dream. But only one of them is worth hearing about in the morning.

FACT #36

Snails

A snail can sleep for three years at a time.

it's  TRUTH 👍

Well . . . technically, they can do a combination of hibernation and estivation.

This is because snails don't like extreme weather. In the winter they hibernate if it's too cold and in the summer they estivate if it's too hot. In fact, in very hot weather, they can secrete mucus to stop them from drying up. That's right, you read that correctly. There could be a snail close by sleeping in its own mucus. But when the weather is just right, snails follow a normal sleeping schedule. Unlike us humans, snails don't follow the rules of night and day. Generally, snails will sleep on and off for periods of 13 to 15 hours.

Afterwards, they get a sudden jolt of energy for the next 30 hours, when they get all their snail chores done.

FACT #37
Rats

In the London Underground, rats will often use the tube to get around because they've learned not to run onto the electrified tracks.

is it TRUTH or POOP?

it's POOP

Thank goodness it's not true. Just imagine sitting in a train carriage next to a bunch of rats reading the morning paper.

There are thousands of rats and mice that live in the many tube systems underneath London. The two rail tracks the trains travel along are electrified, but the little rodents can hop on and off without a single volt passing through them. Why? Because in order to get a full shock, you need to be touching both rails. If someone was to jump on the tracks (definitely not recommended!!!) and balance on one rail, they would be fine. However, if they then lost their balance and touched the floor or walls, some voltage would pass through them and escape. Ouch! For the rats and mice, it's an easy feat to walk along a rail and hop on and off.

So, they have no reason to use the tube, unless one of them decides they'd like to visit a relative in Scotland.

FACT #38
Sharks

You're more likely to be killed by a cow, a vending machine, or by taking a selfie than by a shark.

Oh yes, you read that right. But why? Let me (try to) explain.

When you look at what goes on a death certificate, there are people who have died from getting kicked or stepped on by a cow. But before you vow to never visit a farm again, it's not that many people. It's estimated 20 people die per year at the hooves of a cow compared to 5 people at the jaws of a shark across the globe. Now, let's talk about vending machines. It's an odd one, but when you think about how often have you seen a shark in the wild compared to walking past or using a vending machine. It's the people who try to shake out a free snack that risk getting crushed by the heavy rectangular boxes, which happens to about 13 people per year. And lastly, it's time to question if our phones should be our best friends. It's estimated that 37 people across the globe die every year as a direct result of taking a selfie, and most of them happen in India.

In fact, sharks should be the ones who swim away and hide as humans kill about 100 million sharks per year.

FACT #39

Snakes

Snakes can help predict earthquakes.

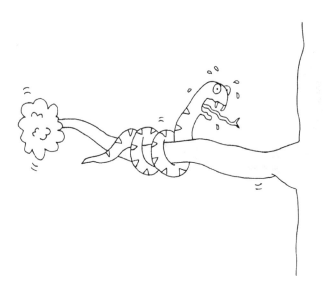

is it TRUTH or POOP?

it's TRUTH

The slithery serpents might be scary (and often poisonous), but it turns out they do have one redeeming quality.

China has a quake zone, or an area prone to dangerous earthquakes. So, it makes sense that the Chinese Government would fund research into predicting when an earthquake will hit. However, I'm guessing they were surprised when the scientists told them they needed to build snake farms. Snakes can sense a coming earthquake from 120 km (75 miles) away, up to five days before it happens. They don't know how they do it, but when they do, they quickly slither out of their nests away from the area and will even smash into walls when trying to escape. There are 12 cities in China that are now being monitored across 143 high-tech monitoring stations. Cameras across the country are watching snakes 24 hours a day.

The nice ending to this crazy snake surveillance fact is that in order to facilitate the camera monitoring the government laid super-fast broadband to remote areas in the country. So, there are now Chinese farmers surfing the internet for the best snake videos on YouTube.

FACT #40

Frogs

There are tree frogs that, instead of hopping, do cartwheels to get around.

it's TRUTH

These clever frogs have out evolved their cousins and learned some brand-new acrobatic skills.

Tree frogs live, yep, you guessed it, up in the trees. This has its advantages, but the biggest danger is falling off a branch to their death. So, the Amazon Milk Frog has toe pads that can hold up to 14 times its own body weight (that's like you or me lifting an average car over our heads). When they fall they do cartwheels in the air, to slow themselves down, and use the toe pad suckers to grab and hold on to a branch or twig. But that isn't the only acrobatic trick they've learned. They can also belly flop like a pro. Researchers used a slow-motion camera to see how the tree frogs land, and it turns out that sometimes, a belly flop onto a branch was just as good as using its super toes.

The next thing these frogs need to evolve is velcro skin so that they can add the dive bomb to their acrobatic repertoire.

FACT #41

Tigers

Tigers laugh when tickled.

it's

Nope, this is complete poppycock! Well, maybe it's not, as it would be hard to argue either way on this one.

There aren't many people brave enough to tickle the belly of a tiger. But it is true to say that animals laugh. Cute animal videos often do the rounds on YouTube and social media. Scientists have found that laughter is an important form of communication in the animal kingdom. It's a way of saying 'only joking' in the same way a growl is a way of saying 'don't you come any closer'. This is called a play signal, and so far, they have documented 65 different species as having their own form of laughter. Only apes and rats laugh in the same way to us when tickled. Darwin noted in his research that chimpanzees would chuckle as they tickled each other and, when rats are tickled, they giggle in ultrasonic squeaks.

So, it's possible that tigers do laugh, just not when tickled, unless you'd like to travel to India and prove me wrong?

FACT #42
Guinea Pigs

In Switzerland, it is illegal to own just one guinea pig.

it's TRUTH

Strange, but it's true.

It's not some old, traditional law from the middle-ages. Or because the pet shops enforce a buy-one-get-one-free policy for small rodents. The real reason is actually rather sweet. Switzerland is known for its strong human and animal rights. As guinea pigs are social animals, they are considered victims of abuse if they are on their own.

So, if you want to be the proud owner of a guinea pig in Switzerland, you're going to need to buy a bigger cage.

FACT #43

Mices

A starved mouse will eat its own tail.

it's  TRUTH

Gross, right! But it's a genuine fact. When mice get the munchies, they munch on themselves.

There are many animals that have the ability to drop a limb. It's not a party trick, it's a defence mechanism. Imagine being chased by a lion. It would be rather helpful if you could pop off your arm, leave it behind and then run off into the distance while the tasty snack you kindly left distracts the lion. Usually, the limb that gets left behind for the predator is the tail, but for the mouse, it's a different story. In the depths of winter, when food is scarce, the little rodents have a tough decision to make: starve to death or eat their own tail. Don't worry, they can live without it, but they can't grow it back. Salamanders and lizards, on the other hand, can grow back their tails and there is a starfish that will regularly detach an arm and grow it back again and again and again.

Like me, I'm sure you'll be checking the next mouse you spot to see if it had to resort to cannibalism.

FACT #44
Roosters

Roosters have inbuilt earplugs.

it's TRUTH 👍

The humble rooster, or cockerel for those in the UK, has some pretty clever biology to stop them from going deaf.

There is a reason that roosters (male chickens) make good alarm clocks. Their crow is very, very loud. That distinctive cock-a-doodle-doo is piercing. In fact, a study showed that their crowing averages over 100 decibels, which is roughly the same as the noise of a revving chainsaw. So, to prevent themselves from going deaf, they tilt their head back when they crow. This covers their ear canal completely serving as a built-in earplug.

To put it in another way, it is like someone is sticking their fingers in the chicken's ears while they are crowing.

FACT #45
Whales

Sperm whales in the Caribbean have an accent.

A decade-long study has found it to be true.

By collecting and analysing over 4,000 whale calls in the Caribbean, scientists have found that all sperm whales produce one particular coda – a pattern of clicks – that identifies the 'speaker' as being from the Caribbean. In fact, just like humans, they also found that young whales take at least two years to master the accent. They babble and gurgle before producing the correct pattern of clicking sounds. Other animals shown to have dialects include rock hyraxes, monkeys, and many birds.

If that doesn't make you click on social media and send a tweet, I don't know what will.

FACT #46
Rabbits

Rabbits can smell emotions like fear and deception in humans, and scientists are therefore attempting to train rabbits to become lie detectors for the police.

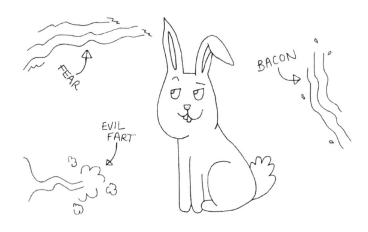

It's, of course, complete and utter nonsense. But a good idea, I hope that you agree.

Just imagine this scene. A hardened criminal sitting in an interrogation room, refusing to give up vital information. The police detective smiles and says, "if you won't talk, I'll have to send in my colleague. And you don't want me to do that." "Do your worst," replies the perp. The door swings open and in hops Fluffy. "No, not that", pleads the frightened criminal. "I promise I don't know anything, just don't let that thing come any closer." The bunny hops onto the metal table and gives the perp a good sniff. Fluffy then turns to the police detective and shakes her head. "Looks like someone's lying. Well done, rabbit interrogator", says the detective as he gives the bunny a carrot and a stroke.

I know, it's so ridiculous it must work. I'll be submitting my research proposal to the police department for £1,000,000 very soon.

FACT #47

Chicks

Chicks can breathe through their shells.

it's TRUTH

This is a cracking fact, and one that shows the animal kingdom can do eggineering (sorry, I'll stop now).

Mammals grow their young in their womb with the umbilical cord connecting the mother to the developing baby. Oxygen-rich blood flows in and carbon dioxide flows back out. So, how do chicks growing in an egg get oxygen? Well, this is where it gets technical. Inside the egg is a 'chorioallantoic membrane'. One end of the membrane is attached to the chick and the other end is close to the eggshell. It connects the chick's circulatory system to the outside world, so in other words, it's like a lung tissue that surrounds the embryo. Oxygen diffuses through microscopic pores in the shell to the blood vessels in the lung, which then flows into the chick's bloodstream. Carbon dioxide, the waste product of respiration, goes out in the opposite direction. Some poor trainee scientist was given the job of counting all the pores and when they were done, they recorded 7,000 of them on one shell (give or take a few).

Amazing, isn't it? A chick can actually breathe through its shell but it definitely can't poop through it.

FACT #48
Worms

Earthworms have five hearts.

it's

Well, depending on your definition of a heart, they either have 0 or 10 hearts.

Earthworms may seem simple because . . . well, look at them, they look like tiny little discarded tentacles. In fact, they have complex inner organs including five pairs of heart-like structures called aortic arches, which they use to pump oxygenated blood to the rest of their bodies. Depending on the definition of "heart", earthworms can be said to have either 10, or zero hearts. Naturalist Charles Darwin famously studied earthworms for over 30 years. Darwin's observations eventually became one of his best-selling books called 'The Formation of Vegetable Mould, through the Action of Worms' (catchy title, I know) which surprisingly sold more copies than his book on Evolution, 'The Origin of Species'.

So, the early bird catches the worm, and we now know that is because the early worm is a very hearty breakfast.

FACT #49
Elephants

Elephants make their very own sunscreen.

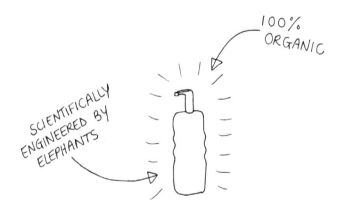

SCIENTIFICALLY ENGINEERED BY ELEPHANTS

100% ORGANIC

is it **TRUTH** or **POOP?**

it's  TRUTH

Turns out that for elephants, taking a mud bath is for more than just having a good time.

Most elephants live close to the equator, which means it's extremely hot for most of the day. After a river or swamp bath, they'll throw mud and sand up and over themselves. Doing so creates a rudimentary sunscreen that protects their skin from the hot, burning sun. Other animals go one step further and have managed to produce a type of sunscreen from their own cells. There is a genetic trait in fish, birds, and reptiles that enables them to produce 'gadusol', which provides protection from ultraviolet rays from the sun. Scientists are even looking into the possibility of humans unlocking the same ability in our skin.

So, which would you choose as a futuristic sunscreen? Fish scales or bird feathers? Personally, I'd join the elephants and opt for the mud bath.

FACT #50
Frogs

There is a frog, hidden deep in the Amazon Rainforest, that has a horn on its head, and an indigenous tribe believe that if you catch one it will grant you a wish.

If anyone reading this book thought this one was a truth, then I'm truly sorry. Cancel those plane tickets to Brazil, because this is codswallop!

In truth, I just really, really wanted to draw a cartoon of a Frog-i-corn – the half-frog, half-uniforn mythical creature from my weird imagination. And I hope you agree, the little critter is magnificent.

So, how many did you get right?

Thanks for reading and I hope you've learnt something new to tell your parents, teachers, friends, and pets.

Please do post how many you got correct as a review (and, while you're there, why not suggest what the theme of the next book should be).

Until next time, happy reading!

About the Author

James Warwood is (usually) very good at writing about himself. So he would like to start by saying that this bio was written on an off day.

He lives on the Welsh Border with his wife, two boys, and carnivorous plant. For some unknown reason he chose a career in Customer Service, mainly because it was indoor work and involves no manual labour. He writes and illustrates children's books by night like a superhero.

Anyway, people don't really read these bios, do they? They want to get on with reading a brand new book or play outside, not wade through paragraphs of text that attempts to make the author sound like a really interesting and accomplished person. Erm . . . drat, I've lost my rhythm.

Discover Other Books by James Warwood

MORE TRUTH OR POOP?

Book One: Amazing Animal Facts

Book Two: Spectacular Space Facts

Book Three: Gloriously Gross Facts

THE 49 SERIES

Non-fiction cartoon series full of helpful tips and laugh-out-loud silliness for getting the most out of life.

The Excuse Encyclopedia: Books 1 - 12 in the 49 Series

THE SKELETON KEYS CHRONICLES

Middle-grade fiction series that's got it all . . . ruthless pirates, epic monsters, legendary adventures

Book One: Monsters of the Sea

Book Two: Back from the Dead Red

Book Three: Admiral of the Black

MIDDLE-GRADE STAND-ALONE FICTION

The Grotty Spoon: The Most Disgusting Restaurant in the World

The Boy Who Stole One Million Socks

The Village Creatures: A Tale About Tails

WHERE TO FIND JAMES ONLINE

Website: www.cjwarwood.com

Facebook Page: James Warwood

Twitter: @cjwarwood

Printed in Great Britain
by Amazon